D0572662

NO LONGER PROPERTY OF
ANYTHINK LIBRARIES/
RANGEVIEW LIBRARY DISTRICT

T1-BLK-607

Quick Expert
Ancient Egypt

Jill Laidlaw

Crabtree Publishing Company
www.crabtreebooks.com

Author: Jill Laidlaw
Editor: Crystal Sikkens
Project coordinator: Kathy Middleton
Production coordinator: Ken Wright
Prepress technician: Margaret Amy Salter
Series consultant: Gill Matthews

Every effort has been made to trace copyright holders and to obtain their permission for use of copyright material. The authors and publishers would be pleased to rectify any error or omission in future editions. All the Internet addresses given in this book were correct at the time of going to press. The author and publishers regret any inconvenience caused if addresses have changed or sites have ceased to exist, but can accept no responsibility for any such changes.

Picture Credits:
Corbis: Bojan Brecelj 11t
Dreamstime: Wormold 13b
Istockphoto: Luke Daniek 6–7,
  Jeremy Mayes various pages, Manuel Velasco 14
Photolibrary: The Print Collector 19
Shutterstock: (Cover) Mirek Hejnicki, Maugli,
  Holger Mette, Dan Ionut Popescu, 10, Kharidehal
  Abhirama Ashwin 13t, Mario Bruno 17,
  Zhu Difeng 16, Pichugin Dmitry 7t, Iconex 8r,
  Vladimir Korostyshevskiy 21, Maugli 11b,
  Luciano Mortula 15, Juriah Mosin 18, Nagib 9,
  Jovan Nikolic 8b, David Peta 5b, Jose Antonio
  Sanchez 20, VanHart 12, Alena Yar 5t
Map: Geoff Ward 4

Library and Archives Canada Cataloguing in Publication

Laidlaw, Jill A
    Quick expert : ancient Egypt / Jill Laidlaw.

(Crabtree connections)
Includes index.
ISBN 978-0-7787-9942-9 (bound).--ISBN 978-0-7787-9964-1 (pbk.)

    1. Egypt--Civilization--To 332 B.C.--Juvenile literature.
I. Title. II. Title: Ancient Egypt. III. Series: Crabtree connections

DT61.L34 2010   j932'.01   C2010-901515-0

Library of Congress Cataloging-in-Publication Data

Laidlaw, Jill A.
    Quick expert--ancient Egypt / Jill Laidlaw.
        p. cm. -- (Crabtree connections)
    Includes index.
    ISBN 978-0-7787-9942-9 (reinforced lib. bdg. : alk. paper)
    -- ISBN 978-0-7787-9964-1 (pbk. : alk. paper)
    1. Egypt--Civilization--To 332 B.C.--Juvenile literature. I. Title. II.
Title: Ancient Egypt. III. Series.

DT61.L253 2010
932--dc22

2010008064

Crabtree Publishing Company

www.crabtreebooks.com   1-800-387-7650
Copyright © 2011 **CRABTREE PUBLISHING COMPANY.**
All rights reserved. No part of this publication may be reproduced, stored in a retrieval system or be transmitted in any form or by any means, electronic, mechanical, photocopying, recording, or otherwise, without the prior written permission of Crabtree Publishing Company. Published in the United Kingdom in 2009 by A & C Black Publishers Ltd. The right of the author of this work has been asserted.

Printed in the U.S.A./062010/WO20100815

Published in Canada
Crabtree Publishing
616 Welland Ave.
St. Catharines, Ontario
L2M 5V6

Published in the United States
Crabtree Publishing
PMB 59051
350 Fifth Avenue, 59th Floor
New York, New York 10118

Contents

Who Were the Egyptians?

Egypt is located in the northern part of Africa. The Mediterranean Sea is on one side and the Red Sea is on the other.

History of ancient Egypt

About 7,000 years ago, ancient Egypt was two separate kingdoms—one at each end of the Nile River. The Nile River flows from the south to the north. The south end was called Upper Egypt. The north end was called Lower Egypt.

About 2,000 years later, Upper Egypt conquered Lower Egypt. For the first time, both kingdoms were ruled by one king—King Menes.

Did you know?

There were 365 days in an Egyptian year—just like our year—but they had ten days in a week!

This map of ancient Egypt shows some of its many important sites.

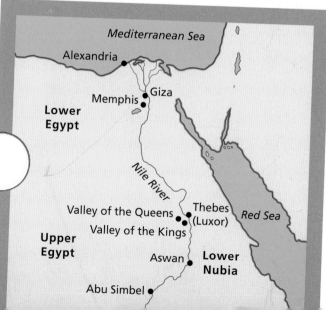

Mediterranean Sea

Alexandria

Memphis • Giza

Lower Egypt

Nile River

Valley of the Queens • Thebes
Valley of the Kings • (Luxor)   Red Sea

Upper Egypt

Aswan   **Lower Nubia**

Abu Simbel •

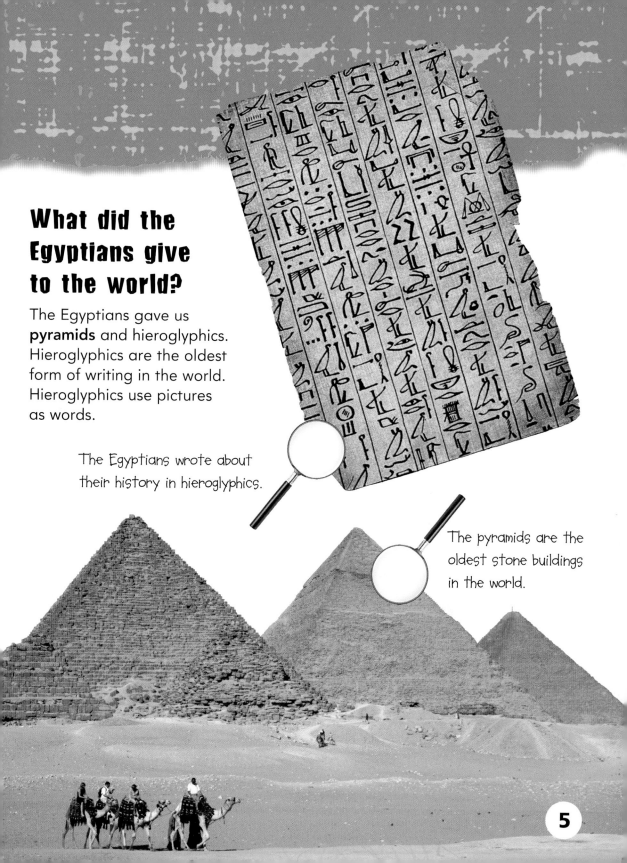

What did the Egyptians give to the world?

The Egyptians gave us **pyramids** and hieroglyphics. Hieroglyphics are the oldest form of writing in the world. Hieroglyphics use pictures as words.

The Egyptians wrote about their history in hieroglyphics.

The pyramids are the oldest stone buildings in the world.

The Nile River

There were not many roads in ancient Egypt. The Nile was the best way to get around. Goods from other lands, such as food and blocks of stone for building pyramids and **temples**, were all carried in boats along the Nile River.

Farming

The Nile was the reason Egypt was so rich. The river flooded every year from mid-June to October. It covered farmland in rich, black mud called silt, which was good for the crops.

Water from the Nile River runs into canals cut into farmland. This brings water to the crops.

Did you know?

The Nile is the longest river in the world—it is 4,184 miles (6,733 km) long.

Food

Crops grown next to the Nile included barley, vegetables, wheat, grapes, beans, garlic, melons, and onions.

People risked being eaten by crocodiles and having their boats overturned by hippos to catch fish from the Nile.

The ancient Egyptians were afraid of hippos, but they also worshiped them.

Irrigation

Water from the Nile was used to feed the soil. The Egyptians built canals between their fields to carry the water to as much land as possible. This is called irrigation.

Trade and the Army

The Nile River was busy with **merchant** ships arriving from other countries and leaving for other ports.

Imports

The Egyptians bought gold, ivory, wood, and animal skins from people in other parts of Africa. They bought olive oil and silver from countries across the Mediterranean Sea and from the **Aegean Islands**.

Exports

The Egyptians sold goods such as grain, **linen**, metals, **papyrus**, wine, and precious stones.

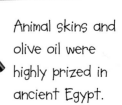

Animal skins and olive oil were highly prized in ancient Egypt.

Archers fired arrows from chariots, as well as on foot.

The army

There were times when the Egyptians did not have an army, and there were other times when the army was large and powerful.

The Egyptian army had archers, **charioteers**, and foot soldiers. They also employed **mercenaries** to fight for them.

Foot soldiers did not have any armor to protect themselves—not even shoes. All they carried were simple bows and arrows, which they used in battle.

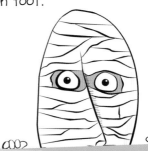

Did you know?

Soldiers grew their hair long to protect their heads—only the commanders had helmets.

Everyday Life

Most Egyptians were farmers. Children worked in the fields, too. When the fields were flooded, people worked for the **pharaoh** building palaces, pyramids, and temples.

Houses

Most people in ancient Egypt lived close to the Nile River. Their homes were built of bricks made from mud that turned hard when baked in the Sun.

Curved blades, called sickles, were used to cut corn.

Did you know?

Many men and women wore wigs, perfume, and makeup.

Schools

Most Egyptians could not read or write. They had to pay to go to school. Schools were mostly for boys, but girls from rich families often went to school, too.

This wall painting shows an ancient Egyptian father with his daughter.

What they wore

Ancient Egypt, like Egypt today, was hot, so people did not wear many clothes. Most children ran around naked. Boys usually had shaved heads with a little ponytail on one side.

Barter

The Egyptians did not have money. People were paid in goods such as food. Then they traded this for other things. This is called bartering.

Some women wore cones of perfumed fat on their heads.

11

Egyptian Gods

The ancient Egyptians worshiped almost 2,000 gods. The gods were usually half-human and half-animal.

The myth of the Sun god

Myths were told about the gods. The Egyptians believed that Amun-Ra, the Sun god, created the world. They thought that Amun-Ra was reborn as the Sun every day and sailed his boat across the sky. Amun-Ra sailed through the **underworld** at night.

Here, the Pharaoh Akhenaton is worshiping Aten—the Lord of Heaven and Earth. Aten became an important god while Akhenaton was pharaoh.

This painting shows Queen Nefertari (far right), the goddesses Maat (far left), Isis (center), and the god Horus.

Some gods

- Horus looked after the pharaoh and had the head of a **falcon**.

- Hathor was the goddess of music, love, dancing, and happiness. She was married to Horus.

- Amun-Ra was the Sun god and had the head of a hawk.

- Osiris was the god of the underworld. He taught the Egyptians to farm.

- Isis was the great mother goddess and was married to Osiris—her brother!

- Anubis was the god of the dead, who guided and protected spirits in the afterlife. He had the head of a **jackal**.

This wall carving shows Horus (left) and Hathor (right).

13

Temples

Ancient Egyptians worshiped some gods at small shrines, or places to pray, they made in their homes.

They worshiped the biggest and most important gods in grand temples. Ordinary people were only allowed to go a little way into the temple. Only priests and the pharaoh could enter the inner temple.

Egyptian priests carry an ark, or boat, made for the god Osiris.

The Temple of Pharaoh Ramses II at Abu Simbel was carved from rock 3,300 years ago.

Temples

The Egyptians thought the gods made the very first temple, so all temples were built to the same plan.

Each temple was dedicated to a different god and had a large statue of him. There was also a statue of the ruling pharaoh.

Many temples were built along the east bank of the Nile River, so that the Sun would rise on them every morning.

Priests

Three times a day, the priests:

- 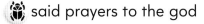 said prayers to the god

- washed and dressed the statue of the god

- brought the statue food

Did you know?

Every day, the priests washed in sacred temple water and shaved their whole bodies.

15

Pharaohs

The word *pharaoh* meant "great house" to the ancient Egyptians. They believed the spirit of the gods lived in the body of the pharaoh on Earth. They also thought that the pharaoh himself was a god. He made all the decisions, and everyone had to obey him. He had two **viziers** to help him.

Headdress

Dynasties

Egyptian history is divided up into periods of time called "dynasties." This is how long each pharaoh's family ruled for.

This pharaoh's headdress has a **cobra's** head. The cobra was believed to protect the pharaoh.

Queens

Pharaohs had one main wife and a lot of other wives as well. Not many people were important enough to marry a pharaoh, so he sometimes married his own sister!

Did you know?

Tutankhamun is one of the most famous pharaohs. He came to the throne at the age of nine and died when he was 19 or 20. Some people think that he was murdered.

This is Queen Nefertiti, wife of Pharaoh Akhenaton.

Mummies

Egyptians believed that their spirits made a journey
to the "next world," or underworld, after their death.
After the spirit had been judged by the god Osiris, it
would return to its body. This meant that Egyptians
believed it was important to keep dead bodies
"fresh" by making them into mummies.

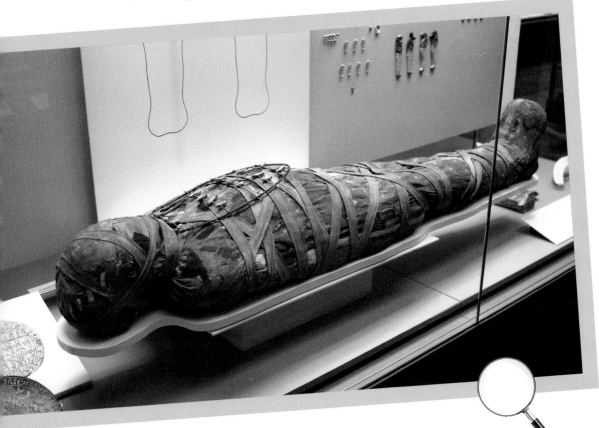

It took about 70 days
to mummify a dead body.

Organs were put in canopic jars such as these.

How to make a mummy

🪲 Wash the dead body.

🪲 Pull out the **organs**, except for the heart, through a cut made in the side of the body. Store the liver, lungs, stomach, and intestines in separate **canopic jars**.

🪲 Pull the brain out of the skull by poking a hook up the person's nose and then throw it away.

🪲 Cover the body in a saltlike powder, called **natron**, and leave it for about 40 days.

🪲 Stuff the body with linen and sawdust soaked in oils.

🪲 Sew up the cut in the side.

🪲 Wrap the mummy in up to 20 layers of linen.

🪲 Place it in its coffin and put a mask over its head and face.

Pyramids

Important or rich people were mummified and buried in massive tombs called pyramids.

How were they built?

No one really knows how the pyramids were built. As far as we can tell, the Egyptians did not have machines to help them.

Teams of builders, **masons**, and workers chipped the enormous blocks of stone for the pyramids out of the ground. Boats were used to transport the blocks along the Nile River. A single block could weigh as much as an automobile.

The biggest pyramid in Egypt is the Great Pyramid, built for Pharaoh Khufu. Its base is the size of eight soccer fields.

What's inside?

There was a burial chamber, or room, in the center of the pyramid. This was for the coffin.

Everything the person would need for the afterlife, such as clothes, chariots, food, furniture, horses, pets, and wine would be put in the pyramid.

The walls of pyramids were often painted with pictures telling the story of the dead person's life, as well as magic spells and pictures of the gods.

21

Glossary

Aegean Islands A group of islands close to, and belonging to, Greece

Canopic jars Jars for keeping the organs from a dead body safe. Each body usually had four of these jars

charioteers Men who drive chariots

cobra A poisonous snake

falcon A type of hunting bird

jackal A type of wild dog

linen The material wrapped around a dead body to form a mummy

mason A skilled worker that builds using stone, brick, or concrete

mercenaries Professional soldiers from other countries

merchant A person who travels to buy and sell goods

myth An ancient story

natron A white/yellow mineral used to preserve dead bodies

organs Important parts of the body such as the heart, the liver, and the lungs

papyrus A type of reed that was cut and pressed into sheets to form A type of writing paper

pharaoh The name given to an Egyptian king

pyramid A tomb shaped like a triangle on four sides, with a perfectly square base

temples Places where people worship gods and goddesses

underworld The place Egyptians believed they went to after they died. The underworld was ruled by Osiris

viziers The pharaoh's most trusted advisors. They helped him to run the country

Further Information

Web sites

Nile facts, both ancient and modern, can be found at:
www.ancient-egypt-online.com/river-nile-facts.html

The Carnegie Museum of Natural History's site about life in ancient Egypt can be found at:
www.carnegiemnh.org/exhibitions/egypt/index.htm

Enjoy puzzles and games about ancient Egypt at:
www.kingtutone.com/kids/

Find out more about life in ancient Egypt at:
www.historyforkids.org/learn/egypt
http://egypt.mrdonn.org/

Books

Ancient Egypt (Passport to the Past) by Philip Steele. Rosen (2009)

In Ancient Egypt (How'd They Do That?) by Tamra Orr. Mitchell Lane Publishers (2009)

Mummy (DK Eyewitness Books) by James Putnam. DK Publishing (2009).

Life in Ancient Egypt (Peoples of the Ancient World) by Paul Challen. Crabtree Publishing Company (2005)

The Ancient Egyptians: Dress, Eat, Write and Play just like the Egyptians (Hands-on History) by Fiona Macdonald. Crabtree Publishing Company (2008)

Index